STEPPING INTO SCIENCE

COLOR

By Illa Podendorf

Illustrations by Wayne Stuart
Product Illustration, Inc.

CHILDRENS PRESS, CHICAGO

Illa Podendorf, former chairman of the Science Department of the Laboratory Schools, University of Chicago, has prepared this series of books with emphasis on the processes of science. The content is selected from the main branches of science—biology, physics, and chemistry—but the thrust is on the process skills which are essential in scientific work. Some of the processes emphasized are observing, classifying, communicating, measuring, inferring, and predicting. The treatment is intellectually stimulating which makes it occupy an active part in a child's thinking. This is important in all general education of children.

This book, COLOR, emphasizes the process of observing. Special emphasis is placed upon recognizing by sight the basic colors in different shades.

Library of Congress Catalog Card Number: 77-159791

1 2 3 4 5 6 7 8 9 10 11 12 13 14 15 16 17 18 19 20 21 22 23 24 25 R 75 74 73 72 71

CONTENTS

RED, BLUE, AND YELLOW

Go on a hunt and find something red.

Did you find a red mitten?

Did you find a red cap?

Did you find a red coat?

Did you find a red shoe?

Did you find a red bird?

Did you find a red wheel?

Did you find a red sled?

Did you find a red nose?

Go on a hunt and find something blue.

9

Did you find a blue shirt?

Did you find a blue shoe?

Did you find a blue ribbon?

Did you find a blue sweater?

Did you find a blue car?

Did you find a blue box?

Did you find a blue wagon?

Did you find a blue jump-rope?

Go on a hunt and find something yellow.

13

Did you see a yellow banana?

Did you see a yellow rope?

Did you see a yellow top?

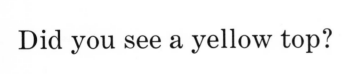
Did you see a yellow cat?

Did you see a yellow pail?

Did you see a yellow coat?

Did you see a yellow sweater?

Did you see a yellow scooter?

These balloons are red. Some of them are lighter red. Others are darker red.

Perhaps you would say that one balloon is pink. We do call that color pink. But it is a light shade of red.

All these toys are shades of blue.

All these toys are shades of yellow.

GREEN, ORANGE, PURPLE

Lisa saw a cart full of vegetables.
The vegetables were all green. But
they were not the same green. Some
were lighter green than others.

Lisa had three crayons—red, yellow,
blue.
Lisa colored a paper-doll dress yellow.
Then she took a blue crayon and colored
over the yellow. The dress was green.
Try it. Can you make green by coloring
yellow over blue?

The leaves on these plants are green.

Find the two green mittens.

Lisa had two things in her lunch box
that were an orange color. Find them.

Lisa is making a picture of the orange
in her lunch box. She is using her red
and yellow crayons.

Lisa drew other orange-colored things. These are the pictures that Lisa made. First she used her red crayon. Then she colored yellow over the red.

Could you use the yellow color first, and then the red? Try it.

Some of these flowers are orange.
But they are not all the same shade
of orange.

Lisa saw some purple flowers.
Some were lighter purple than others.

Lisa passed a store window.

All the clothes in the window were purple, or they had some purple on them.

Lisa had only red, blue, and yellow watercolors. She wanted to make a purple dress for her paper doll. She found a way to do it.

See the next page.

Lisa mixed red and blue to make purple for the paper doll dress.

Lisa had found that with just red, yellow, and blue paints she could make green, orange, and purple, too.

CIRCLE OF COLOR

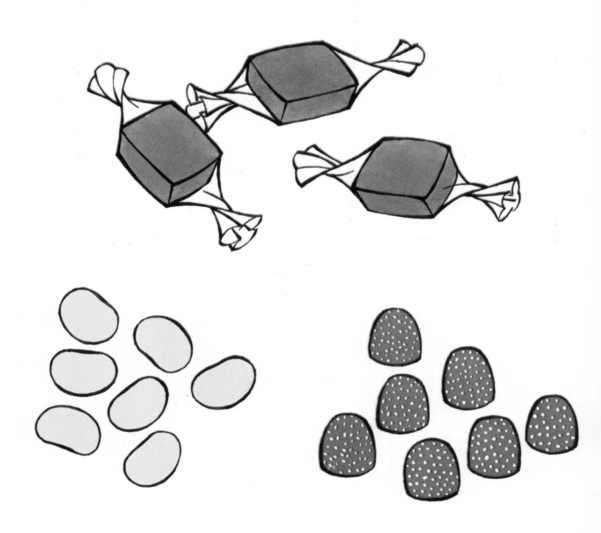

Here are candies of three
different colors. What are they?

Here are candies of four colors. What
are they? Can you think of a reason
for placing the green between the blue
and the yellow?

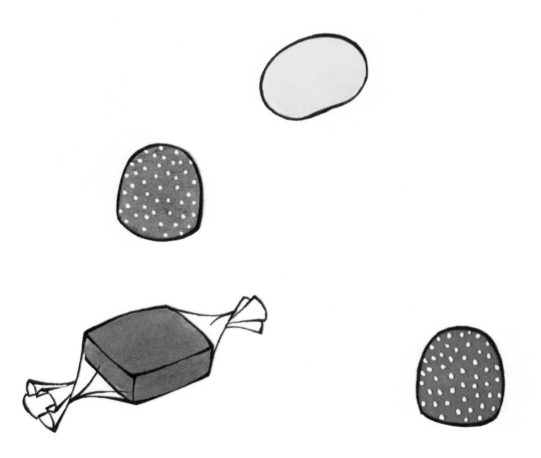

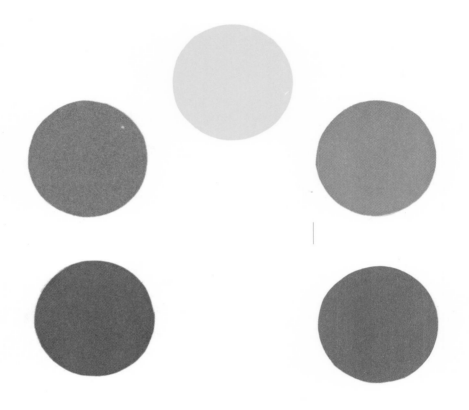

Here are five colors. What are they?

Can you see why the orange is placed where it is?

What is a color that is missing?

Where could it be placed?

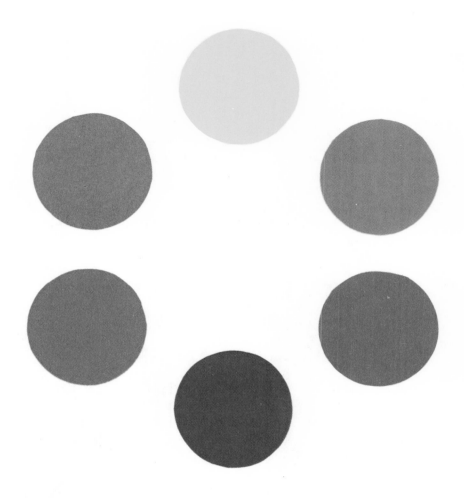

Now there are six colors. Is the purple placed where you would have put it?

BROWN

Jeff had red, yellow, and blue paints.

He knew how to mix blue and yellow to make green.

He knew how to mix red and yellow to make orange.

He knew how to mix red and blue to make purple.

But Jeff wanted to paint some horses. He did not want red, yellow, blue, green, orange, or purple horses.

He wanted BROWN.

He mixed some red, blue,
and yellow. He had brown.

He painted some horses. He made them light brown and dark brown.

He painted some deer.

COLORS ALL AROUND US

These kittens have more than one color.

How many colors can you find?

How many colors can you find
among the leaves?

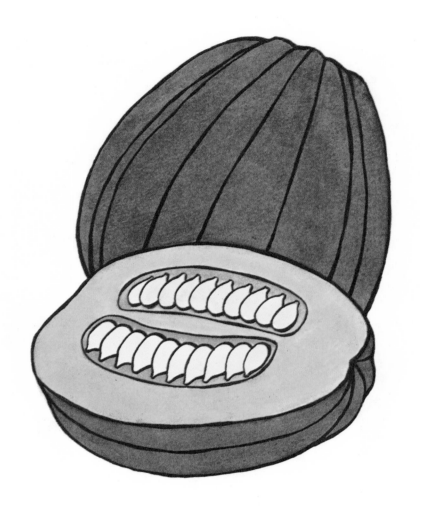

How many colors can you see
in this picture of a squash?
Which color is on the outside?
Which colors are on the inside?

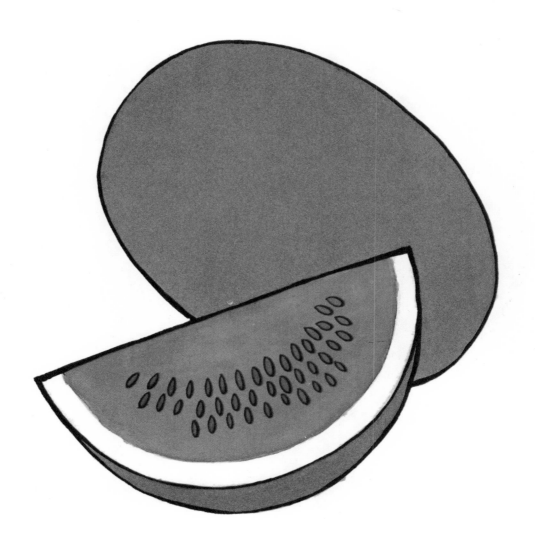

How many colors can you see
in this picture of a watermelon?
Which color is on the outside?
Which colors are on the inside?

Would you like to eat the apples
from this tree? What does the green
color tell you about these apples?

Would you like to eat the apples from this tree? What does the red color tell you about these apples?

What does the red
in this picture
say to you? You
are sure to know
that it says STOP.

What does the yellow
in this picture say to
you? WAIT? LOOK?

What does the green
in this picture say to
you? Does it say GO,
if all is clear?

What does the green
arrow say? Does it say
GO THIS WAY?

SOME THINGS TO DO

Use your red, yellow, and blue crayons in as many ways as you can. How many colors were you able to get?

Use your red, yellow, and blue watercolors. Could you get the same colors as you did with the crayons? Can you get other colors?

Find how many different greens you can get by using blue and yellow.

Find out how many shades of orange you can get with red and yellow.

Find out how many shades of purple you can get with red and blue.

Can you find ways to get light and dark red, blue, and yellow?